I0765105

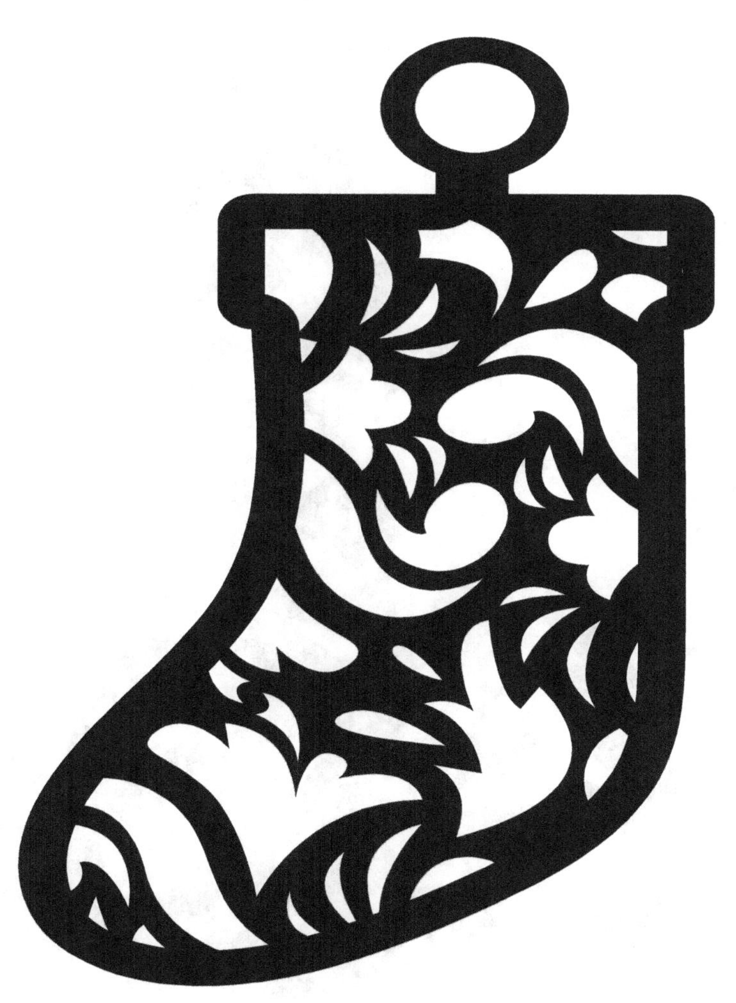

jesus
is the
reason

Joy

Happy
New
Year

joy
Love
Peace

merry n' bright

Merry
Christmas

Let It
SNOW

CHRIST
IS BORN

PEACE
LOVE
JOY

BLESSED

PEACE

LOVE

MERRY

FAITH

JOY

NOEL

PEACE
on
Earth

Jingle Bells

Be
Merry

JOY
to the
world

Let it
Snow

Be
Jolly

Holy
Night

Believe
in the magic

merry
&
bright

MERRY
CHRISTMAS

CHRISTMAS 2020
Masked & Merry

O, Holy
Night

BLITZEN • RUDOLF • DASHER • DANCER • PRANCER • VIXEN • COMET • CUPID • DONNER •

merry
&
bright

MY
FIRST
Christmas

PROUD
member
OF
THE
NAUGHTY
LIST

Joy

MERRY
Christmas

THE MOST
Wonderful
Time
OF THE YEAR

The Year of the Lockdown
2020
Merry Christmas

www.ingramcontent.com/pod-product-compliance
Lightning Source LLC
Chambersburg PA
CBHW081559270726
48657CB00029B/3381